HOW TO OPEN A BOOK OF POETRY

Sidle up to it
as if it were a thigh
you've wanted to stroke
every night for the last
few light-years.

BY TERRY STOKES

Natural Disasters 1971

Crimes of Passion 1973

Boning the Dreamer 1975

BONING THE DREAMER

Alfred A. Knopf, New York, 1975

BONING THE DREAMER

Terry Stokes

THIS IS A BORZOI BOOK
PUBLISHED BY ALFRED A. KNOPF, INC.

 Published in the United States by Alfred A. Knopf, Inc., New York, and simultaneously in Canada by Random House of Canada Limited, Toronto. Distributed by Random House, Inc., New York.

* * *

The author wishes to thank the following magazines in which some of the poems in this collection first appeared: *Aisling, Broadway Boogie, Confrontation, Cross Country, CutBank, Four Quarters, Gravida, The Greenfield Review, Isthmus, New Letters, Next, Poetry Now, Rapport, Second Coming, Sotto Voce, The Times Literary Supplement, Words;* and the following, which have published some of the poems as broadsides or booklets: The Bellevue Press, Cold Mountain Press Postcard Series, *Diana's Bi-Monthly* Broadside Series, The Hearsay Press, *Some* Broadside Series, The Visual Studies Wordshop.

The author is grateful to the Creative Artists Public Service Program for a grant which helped in the completion of this book.

LIBRARY OF CONGRESS CATALOGING IN PUBLICATION DATA
Stokes, Terry. Boning the dreamer.
I. Title.
PS3569.T622B6 811'.5'4 75-8255
ISBN 0-394-49885-2
ISBN 0-394-73100-X pbk.

Manufactured in the United States of America

First Edition

For Linda Gutstein

CONTENTS

BONING THE DREAMER

BECAUSE WE MUST LOVE OUR TWINS

I groan in the room without you, sister.
I wish you would come home from that long
sexy date, & hold me in your arms. I
listen to the ball game, late, in Los
Angeles. A single kicks off the second
baseman's mitt: the winning hit.

Several years later, someone would suggest
an orgy, & I would think of you cuddled up
in the back seat of a semiautomatic sedan.
Your pants around your knees, your heart
stuck to the drifting car radio. I would
wonder at the number of fingers we cart around.
They aren't enough.

I crawl into that soft deathbed with you,
& brew a tea few people can swallow
without stirring, sorting the dark leaves first.

THE SHORT-SIGHTED MATRON OF MERCY

Since the black dog's death,
we haven't been able
to get our names straight.

We stare at the soiled orange dishes
in the sink. We sleep until
we can praise our nightmares.

At thirty, I am as angry
as I was at eight, sliding
into the coal bin; locked out

again. My stepfather has left
the key in the wrong place, & I
scream through the red spiders

in the cellar. Black dust rises;
the wicked fuel for someone's fire.

THERE I AM

ten or fifteen years
later, crouched in the loose
bathing suit waiting
for the sun to finally
appear. No point in it,
someone said, with a foolish
head for business & a seersucker
suit, apparently. I said, this isn't
something you fool around with, this
is out of context, & I've been trying
to get back to that forever. He went
on someplace, what exactly was the pain
in sitting down with a few words handy,
& a lot of gall all ready to be tapped?
The typewriter is a wonderful machine,
lots of surprises, & a genuine sense
of broken tables.

2 *There I Am*
ten or fifteen years
later, eating a Mars bar
on a sticky day, & wondering
who stuck the snake in the Coke
machine, & why the cops came
smiling to my house to talk about
the Coke machine & its problems. I
have problems of my own. Where to
keep the Coke, & yet, I don't want
anything on my permanent record. I want
my record to look like a windmill
smiling in the sunset. I go in for
space travel, & the diseases one
can incur. My fingers unravel
with Athlete's Foot. Look, I'm
bound to the cement tooth, &
the grind of late, cheap nights
eating out the heart of transistor,
some fire room in a luxury building.

3 *There I Am*

ten or fifteen years
later, driving a bloodless
car into downtown Sicily, & worried
about income tax, & my lack of
understanding of nonprofit
business. I push a few people
against a wall & ask them for
all they're worth. Always a short
change in this lousy deal. I bump
off an old friend or his
mother. & then, somebody
wants a kneecap job done
on their grandfather. I am
goodness, & light, & reject
nothing. I pour pythons
into children's dreams, & they
don't know how to spend the time.
I gleam like an axle, my
old father's striking face. Push
the car in second gear
up a broken mountain. There aren't
any more broads to fix the breakfast,
& the sheets are cardboard honeys
doing cartwheels, backbends, & one
can do something that's hard to
describe. She's a chip of rose
paint, & wavers this whole
night, a shadow of her former self.
A shadow of her former self.

4 *There I Am*

ten or fifteen years
later, I restore a house
in Queens. I go out onto
the piazza, & play with the glass
straws, & the green wicker furniture.
This is where she smelled of fish;
this is where she paused to cool
herself, her twelve children. Her
garden stakes, green, prod my
arches. She is, after all, a good
woman, & it has taken me a hundred
years, to find her book, & the windows
of that book. The fact that she
wanted everyone to be as regular;
the fact that she was frightened of her
husband's bowel blood; the fact
that every time she emptied her mouth
she killed someone
who looked like her sister. These are
not things you can do with a house.
Or a yellow V-neck sweater
she gives you the money for. Nothing
here, but a collapsible card table,
& thin green gospel records
floating on a phonograph
on that piazza of green straws.

5 *There I Am*
ten or fifteen years
later, I smash flies
& frogs with a croquet mallet.
I hit the balls thru the wickets,
thru the summer, under the white
fence, onto the newly tarred road.
It is slime week in the country. It
is a week of sandy thighs,
& dirty brook water for baths. I
can feel them coming on. The week
of scouring pads, & bent spikes.
The week of endless foul balls. The
week of poetry about typewriters. The
week of my stepfather's shit
in the toilet. The week of the smell
that lingers. The week of hanging
bleeding thumb, & the week of the
bleeding knuckles. The week of
the burning tree house, & the child
who burns within.

6 *There I Am*
ten or fifteen years
later. I kiss my elbow
on a butcher block. & that
starts the whole chain of
dreams. A hammock hung in pines,
fireflies lift me toward the moon.
The kissing bug, bites, kisses
my lips, an old friend
paid to put me away for a while.

MASKS

FOR JAMES WRIGHT

The proper pills keep me
from cracking my head in the shower,
& the mess expected therein.

The Chinese child stretches her head
over the booth in The Great Shanghai.
She does not speak as I would not speak.

I collect the scars of limited travel
on my face, a devil mask for me alone.
I squint from the eyeholes, & welcome

everyone home. Bumbling, foolish, I,
too, watch this shadow of a heart
leap from the landscape to some place

we can only know when we
dive from a dark boat out of love.

LAYING CLAIMS

1 So, all your young life you
spend writing to beat the mother

from your tubes, & gradually, you
phase her out, a Renault Dauphine,

a beer without gusto, & move
on, a Country & Western dude with

his cherrywood hummingbird
guitar. Now, there's a man of few

words. & he says it without accompaniment.
These are all virtues you can

face up to in the morning. The baggy
blue socks stuck over your funny hands.

Oh, it's just finding a cliché who'll
marry your fingers. All of them, at

once, starved for attention.

2 I don't like this poetry of cramps, &
smooth palms. Lines knotted to

one another. A slow puff adder believed
to be very venomous, or not venomous.

To see morning in this place is to grow,
tired, arms, squeezed lemons on the

drainboard, & no one about to clean without
charging toward you, the splintered bookcase,

& my first name. The phone rings
spray off the walls, cornered cats

drifting into your heart.

3 Some days even your footprints
need splints to hold up

under the strain of the blunt sky.
Some days your eyes are foster children

running away. To the general store
with the money you saved in the red

coffee can. A couple of pennies
worth a nickel; one, minted in

the backyard near the imported
lawn chair. Some days the belly

hangs on every bite, & refuses.
The system a sprinter out breaking

all records. Some days the knees
quiver for the hell of it all.

Some days the navel bleeds for a hundred years
as it discovers it's been sitting, a bulging

quiet noodle, the same skin, half a century,
alone, to trust no one, to trust no one.

4 The quick, breathless widow isn't finished.
She shimmies in the blood. Neat, cured. In

a place this large the wood scars spread
this unbroken whisper. Knock off another

year. This is a song about how to
die. A piece of hospital light for

a poem entering the emergency ward. I
have always asked others to bar the

windows, cut down their needs. I drag
my penis in at this point. Hush, a

president with a deep feeling for
flagrant abuse. A lot of back work

scatters on his hard desk; never dries.

5 This lean piece of meat, this shudder
music, chugs thru my slender colon. A

bored soup of foreigners, snapping photos,
& suggestions. I am crazy with tooth

logic, & the glass women of psychic
prisons, mothers who sell their sons

for riddles, read their lovers as stars,
faithless tripping over their sidewalks

of moan. I climb on their kisses of hot
flak, the tokens touched up here &

there. I will fork over my orange Indian
paintbrush for the pink junket. An even

trade. That settles it. I drink the Scotch
cordial Kelly brought to christen this place,

& an angry stomach, & a yen to fabricate
stories instead of poems. I would like

the local éclair maker to give me the stuff
I need. Eight hundred & fifty cakes, he

says. & most with a touch of that old Nazi
chocolate. I believe poems should have some

political roots, but I'm not so sure. Oh,
how sweet the fleur-de-lis on the wallpaper

must be. I'm getting long-winded, & scared.
Peeling goes on, & that's as important as a

tumble from a B-52, another close friend
rumbles up the stairs, & asks maybe for

a little food, a splash of something stiff.
Ah, brother, mother, I am landing, & refuse

to turn your dizzy, blue songs into dust. I
must, I feel, reclaim this life you sold

one Sunday afternoon, a tag sale, the green
lawn, mowed, & trimmed with such devotion.

A SPEECH, FORGIVE ME

FOR MY SISTERS

Rain, & the bug sweat, oh,
my sister, today, you came
into the raw room

with the news, you didn't
know what they do, say
about your intrusion into

what had bothered them most,
their fathers, they called, their
lovers. They had no brothers,

brothers to speak of. No friends,
or eyeteeth. I don't admire this
poetry of sick blood. I don't

miss your father of pale cars,
gutted sewing machines, &
thumping televisions. He is

wandering in the next room, changing all
our worn-out tubes.

IN LIEU OF A FATHER

I have taken up with women
the hysterical walls convey.

I have done the fandango with
some of the shy corners of the earth.

I find myself brave after two drinks,
or two nights without drinking. I create

worlds where two people fuck all the time;
in love, in haste. I have wasted this world,

& would waste any other.

THE GOOD FRIEND

1 To speak as the lemon comments in sleep.
I push toward the slow cats of

disaster. Open their arms, work my
way in. "Let me tell you, you

were warm without effort. No one
asked for anything. Not the old

nickel, not the tidy room, not the
whiplash." The child marching to the

drugstore with two words, & the "Feed
Me," I continue to distribute.

2 I am the haunted child stuck
in the attic of a Cape Cod house.

There's a fortune I can't collect
until I'm a few years older. I am

a shrinking violet, & a fish of broken scales.
A wino with jade nails. I find comfort

in girdles, & how they keep you in shape.
I am the shapely haunted child. My fists,

kissed by my mother, find my good friend's
stomach. The stomach of the future

is in pain; has lost its wind. The fist
of the spine is timeless, self-concerned.

It loses its mind, stumped by the sprained
wrist of the heart. The vicious haunted child

is never frightened, except in the company
of the good friend. Then, the foggy notions

chew mother's fingers until something snaps.
You remember the other person in this poem,

she can figure it out; this crooked, clenched
hand.

3 The good friend takes up where
an arm is dislocated. The good friend

has a mother, too, who knows how the snow
comes again; how the snow signs its old

name on feeling. My grandmother bound
by her money plants, her jade, her cuttings.

Some of these properties the good friend
has noticed as they lie around in my mother's

house. Like Indian-head pennies, I am lying
there. Several Maine coon cats have wound

up their evening on my chest. They breathe
on the good friend, & we will leave shortly

with the aid of oxygen masks, & tears. The
collection agency takes back the limbs, the

sins, the portraits of railroad stations, the
tombstone Sundays, & the scribblings, you call

our lives. We are the only passengers on a bus
from Suffern to Paramus, & we drink the single

beer, & estimate the money, & the time. We are
crossing the cold bridge. There is an analyst

on the other side; he will not be waiting up.
He will sleep in a carriage bed. His dreams

flooded with honeysuckle, tits, and the flat
bread of the haunted, always hungry, child.

The cracked ceilings, & folks dropping in
to make off with the autograph albums, the boxing

records, round by round, the manager muttering,
"Kill the bastard, kill the bastard, put

the kid thru the ropes."

4 The good friend is left to herself
more often than the asparagus fern.

Her hair touches up the air like
seeds in a catalogue of antiques.

This is how people dismiss each other;
this is how they wish to hold hands.

I am faithful to the good friend; I
do not see her often. I am not

frightened when the pills frighten
the snakeskins, the fucking pillow,

the thin rings of my marriage. &
these pictures fill my cuticles, & I am

struck here, staring, a commemorative coin,
spraying the plants with water, again,

again, & they stay moist, & fall. Soon,
I go back to work trimming the roots.

5 In the center of that sky of snow, an otter
is eating a cloud. It belongs to the good

friend. She is harping on old times. They
are angelic, mysteries of the deep. I lounge

in Sweden, compiling suicide notes. Bracing
myself against *Fear;* a sturdy animal loose

in my night eyes, in my creaking ankles. I
go about my business; drag fur thru

the darkness like a man who has worked his way
up. A man who has found his hands

below the ice; turtle eggs rolling over
his palms, & the lines of those palms

give off nothing of the life. The eggs float
downstream like Ping-Pong balls, like memories.

I push my head into that hole; discover
the atmosphere, the perfect air for my love.

THE RIDE

We took the train & ended up
with no one in our pockets.

We scratched thru sleep, & held
on to the stiff drinks.

A mountain of dirty socks
in my head, spins dry.

We moved on to dreams
in the fields of dark animals,
"I can't speak like this anymore."

This morning, & every morning, your
eyes wear rings, & they will not
turn green. All weekend

the fire from the homeland rose;
spontaneous islands still flicker.
& what you passed from your stomach

returns, a flatcar of broken children
lurches into the quiet cave.

THE VOYAGERS

I am fighting for my livelihood.
I am fighting to keep my head above
the waves of the tub. The endless

goddess of wind, she wraps herself
around my waist, & I wander the cluttered
night without a piece of bread to bulge

my stomach. I am fighting with my throat
of anger, & fighting down the threats
of glaciers, & fighting down their friends.

The obvious voices ascend, drop off when
I am ready, & willing. I touch
your shoulder with my radiation hands.

You break up, & we have done it again, as
always, crossed ourselves against the fathers
who draw parables from their dreams.

THE CARNAGE OF MY FAMILY

My family, when clearly mapped,
dangles like a ghost-flower on a cactus.

They left England to rediscover themselves
maiming Indians. They went in

for dangerous sports. If, however, you follow
the trail of the other side of the family

you come across stooped people picking
potatoes, first in Ireland, then, miraculously,

from the cool sand of Long Island. Popping out
eyes, snapping their dirty fingers.

POETRY

I want a poetry so calm, clean, quiet,
I will trip over it as I sleep.

BONING THE DREAMER

1 He gets carried away by
a flock of salivating shepherds.
They look down upon him with eyes,
knotted fish, & soggy bread. They
are not careful of his head, it
bounces on the ground. Five years
old doing somersaults in a marble
quarry trying to get
his father's approval. *That* hurts &
That hurts. They get where they are
going, they drop him. They go into
the bar, order four shorties, thirsty,
most of the beer spills onto their peach fuzz.
He lies like a worn-out scumbag, "Oh,
where have I been that I come to this.
The sun in the middle of my day, ants
licking my pupils." Inside they say, "Once
when I was fourteen, & once when I was twelve,
& once when I was forty-six, & once when
I was eight."

2 On any other day of the week, a hornet flies
up his nose, figure eights in the sinus
passages. His mother's arms, she blows
in his ears. A midget shadowboxes
before a large crowd gathered behind
his eyes. "Who'll take on the midget
for ten bucks?" She climbs into the ring
wearing a red & blue satin bathrobe, "The Mauler,"
stamped in gold letters on the back, something
she picked up in the dressing room. An old
trick, she sticks a thumb into the midget's
right nostril, cramps in his short legs, his
feet, trotters at the early evening track
wearing rubbers three sizes too large. He
wishes for a toothpick, & some salami

to go along with it. He is having problems
breathing, & bad weather can grow anywhere.
The moon eclipses fully in his stomach, someone
in the crowd goes crazy, & connects the midget's
freckles with a Magic Marker, a red one. It
is a woozy lizard. Mother takes the ten
dollars, the woozy lizard, & heads for Tampa,
the next stop on the circuit.

3 He says he has had enough. He wants swimming
in the cellar. He wants to eat the flies off
the dying wood. He wishes he had a taste of
thick rain water. He is not alone with his
smile of stupid dignity. Varnishing floors
until he can see beyond poverty-stricken
germs. "When I am in the wrong room, I do
not think of the walls, or the children of
the rats, my loud voice, or my nervous testicles.
I think only of Startooth, & the way she lowered
herself upon me like a trampoline mat. She
climbed on, & did, over & over again, the back
flip. She would not speak & she would not
moan. & if she had anything to say she did not
say it. When she was through, & sweated
a great deal, I could smell her thighs, rusted
water, she rolled up the mat, red rubber, &
forced it into her throat. She blew me
a kiss good-bye, the red hollow thigh in her
throat complimented her blue suede suit. She
was lovely, lonely, I suspect, & hasn't been
seen since." He is a warm person in a warm
cellar. "Does a fart constitute longing, or
the absence of longing? Do we always become
the wafer for our mother's tongue?" Polishing,
scraping the skin of wood with his bare hands,
finishing off the stray birth places.

4 He drives like a maniac. His white
Chevy. He passes thru the oncoming
car. It's a total wreck. The women
scream like stiff phantoms. & the
first time out. The other car turns
into red velvet in the rear-view mirror.
Against the deep green of the pines. He
suspends himself in the mirror for a
moment, & pushes the dying car on home.

5 Knitting & purling, praying over
the footsteps. A nodule of disease
behind his ear gives him something
to play with. Working together, they
fabricate a house. The bath, loose, falls
onto the lawn, someone else's property. You
must walk thru their accumulation of filth
in the morning after coffee. So much of what
was anticipated passes. Water disappears.
The living room, it lists, Grand Rapids black.
The antique collectors rub their stomachs
on the soft walls, & "Uhmm," "Ah," "Oh,"
what they had in mind. Moths, trapped
in the lethal yarn, dust of wings
brushed away, their eyes, yellow pins
in small dark windows. The hands are
useless & move. A voice as thick as
summer melon shows up. It will not
leave its body.

6 Startooth, you are hungry
on the best day of your life.

A crane pulls from you, your
favorite child.

7 She gives you a headstone for your birthday.
You smile, & "Thank you
so much." She is happy,
you can tell, she has
found just the right gift.
You down it in center field,
Yankee Stadium. The seventh-
inning stretch. In the men's
room, you piss on your small
hard fingers.

8 The father, pilot's license
in hand. The sky was aluminum
foil, "A day like this, makes
you want to take off." Another
family outing inside the mustard
jar. & the stained old goof,
"On to Lakehurst." I was a kid,
but I got the drooling picture.
An orange-juice can & ground
control, "You've just been blown
from the face of the earth." As
he fell apart, I offered a swig
of hemlock, I offered him arsenic
& old lace, I offered him the sweet
water of my bones. "Make me
a wine spritzer," & the bar-
tender's been trying to fix it up
ever since.

9 Startooth removes the shattered
light bulb, replaces it, & climbs
back to sleep.

10 “You soak the fish for three or four
days, until the scales become dandruff.
The fluid should look like a good
scalp massage. Perhaps its eyes
float, gumball soup. That’s good,
too. You place him on the drip board,
carefully, slice with a penknife,
from the tail to the voice box. Don’t
be frightened, he won’t kick up a
storm. Look around, poke a bit. Wear
rubber gloves. See where he keeps
his food. Remove the spine & the
rib cage. O.K., slap him back
together. The blue yarn, stitch
in a hernia or appendix scar. Make
his eye sockets attractive, you don’t
want him to look as tho he’s had an accident,
or been handled imperfectly. Settle
into a bed of parsley on a silver platter,
& let your friends admire, & eat. They
will say, ‘You put your whole life
into this meal.’ ”

11 He shit for nine years without accumulation.
He grasped all the issues
of the day, provided answers
for the filing cabinet of hysteria.
Stomach X-rays occasionally to make sure
there was something left. He surrounded
himself
with his own lower intestine, colon,
spasms, & bleeding penis. He taped
the negatives to his bathrobe, “My
clouds, I walk thru you, & you
come back, ghost-dogs hunting
for the cracks in winter.”

12 Two apartments. One for dreams & one
for tossing salads & ironing clothes.
One for search & one for dinner. One
for death & one for serving. You can
lug your tears thru both, & there will
be little alarm. There is
a vat, & a braided line
you can reach, if there is
no interference, the cold
food. Drain off the surface, pour
into a kidney dish. You will use
this later for basting. Startooth
fumbles with the essential equipment. Draws
a blank in the recipe, crosses
her thick arms close to her body. I reach
into the refrigerator & cannot tell
the hard-boiled eggs from the uncooked
eggs. I cannot tell Easter & Thanksgiving.
Food struts in the book of ingredients,
wind-up toys in the clawing windows. "Watch
the miner with his pick, cradle the foolish
doll, take a chance on the lemons, suck
the twilight between the toes, & a security
deposit, a damage deposit, & something
for my friends." There are dimples
to be licked, bones to reset. I am
open to anything. Startooth hums,
"Food is life, is kelp, is rest, is
dawn, is bubbles, is sand
in the morning." I rinse her hands
with a disinfectant, & prop open
her teeth with large coins. This is
a broken tooth, & this is where
the root begins. "Dead milk
in my mouth," she gurgles.

13 Dusk, & the drive-in movie. A bay
window, winter. His body wobbles
in the projector's light. His neck
is a loose rope. You pan his face,
the noose, & cut him down. You call
the doctor, all the oxygen in the town
has been spent. You give him mouth-to-
mouth, the kiss of life, your
breath. He comes back, "I disfigure
everyone around me. I take their clothes,
their books. I disguise you when I see
you. You are tables, raw tables, you
are fireplaces, you are unicycles, &
sparse trees. When I touch your arms,
snow tires roll toward my heart.
Washed-out roads, & bad cars. No
drinking water in the summer. Jump
starts, someone's always got to push
you when it gets cold. The rest
you'll see for yourself." There
is nothing like blood, & there is
nothing unusual. We call
each other names, we purchase
the right tickets, wear
the light gray coat. & whatever shows
up, screams, the fibers of the fingers,
the dull bone screen.

14 I stroll back, ten years, onto
the slick floor, the "Spotlight"
dance. Her disassociated shoulders,
& hips. I can't believe I don't
know this one. She is dying to have me
do it with her. Have I done it
with her before? Have we thrown
ourselves onto the locked trunk

of an old rusted Ford? Was she
ever a mink, pulled from me by her father
before I passed on? Her lips
move, & she syncs the lyrics. Will
her father ever catch up to her? Will
she tear the heart from the song? Will
I service her without respite? My head
falls, & still she pursues it. I am picking
it up. I go to a doctor who
stitches it up. Success. We start
again, our feet move like crazy. The yellow
ribbon in her hair. I am eating it.
It is good. For a long, long
time.

15 Startooth, & her identification bracelets.
Her tricky scrawl. I never
learn them. Hitching

a ride out of the dead brown pines.
A tent trailer, a dust cover,
take me in. Now, back up, run
her down, run her over. The flecks

of silver glitter
in the hot tar. I do, I will
ride shotgun, Startooth.

DEALING

The eggs were good, filling that morning.
I know you won't forget the eggs. They slid
around in the pan like an old forest. You
said, Hansel & Gretel could never go near
their parents for fear of being burned, or
someone's soufflé. Even tho I am within
striking distance, don't wait up.

The key ring flew out of my hands, & scared
the parquet floor. It clanged, & I answered
the door. Or the people. I seem to be locked
out of my office. If you turn this page, I
will sink into the binding; push, pry, reek
with the glue of nameless people.

I have borrowed your bookcase, sister. You have
borrowed something fitting. I will summer in
Nairobi; you will move into the fresco, winter
in bas-relief. I eat a ham sandwich, & carefully
the mustard slides out of the bread, here now,
on my pants. I will winter in the Bay of Pigs.

Take my hand, we can always visit mother.

THE SECOND-STORY MAN

Death toys with me
like a second-story man.
First, he cases the joint,
then, as he senses the room
is ripe, he kicks a hole in
the only screen left.

On good days, you use a lot of words.
& I allow melancholy, & serrated wings.
Oh, the rugged land is rotten with corn;
the slumber party is about to begin.

COFFEE

1 There is a dark pit
in your pink stomach.
Feed it lime slices. Feed it
sand.

2 There is some slime
asleep in the closet, remember
to speak up when you wish to touch it.

3 & it was a midget with damp fingers
who stole the tendons, & it was
a midget who speeded up the brain,
& it was a midget who filled up
the dry cup.

4 Some stiff water.
Some stiff water, minerals,
vitamins, riboflavin.

5 You will think of the grounds, sparse,
where we all lived like termites.
You will think of the grounds
as they fall through the stainless-steel
basket.

6 The gutted basket comes home.
It visits you for thirty minutes
every day, sitting in the old rocker.
You welcome it as you would
any child on probation.

7 Does it only seem this dark?

8 I buy a load of gravel, & I chain
myself to it. There is a certain
madness to all purchases. It is
like unwelcome coffee.

9 You want not. You weep not. You
wheel around in the crusty chair,
a coffee bean casually bleeding.

10 The liberated coffee
will never perk. We will
wait up.

11 My bones whine with your coffee, love.

CAR

1 Stand on the side of a major highway
& count the number of cars that have mudflaps.
Keep this number in your head for
the rest of the day. Write to General Motors
& tell them everything you have learned
about cars.

2 Prepare to get into a car other than your own.

3 Think of ways to keep cars from stalling.
Think of ways to keep cars from starting.
Think of ways to move cars around like mice.
Think of something like cars.

4 Fall asleep on the hood of a car
in the middle of a large city. Fall
asleep on the trunk of a car in a small
town. Fall asleep on the top of a car
in a showroom.

5 Push a car until you feel like
a mushroom.

6 Ask your parents to give you a car, a truck,
a bus, a motorbike. Then ask them if
they believe in America; ask them if
they love you more than anything.

7 As if you were a doctor, tell a car it
is going to die. See what it does about it.
Ask it if it believes in euthanasia, reincarnation,
the redemption of the soul, the last
sacraments, or astral projection.

8 Cover the car in suitable fabric.

SOME TAKES

1 Does anyone remember what it was like
to be *that* tired? Your chin against
a fatigued window. What if you continue
to love everyone you've ever loved. &
she is smiling at you with those buckteeth,
& blanched freckles, & talking about
horses forever. It is a room stocked
with bathing beauties; the styles of the suits
change gradually, & you reach, you finally
fondle the elastic breasts.

2 It is a washed-out rainbow, titled,
appropriately, "Blue Meat Loaf—it
went out in the rain & didn't put its
coat on." That is life for you:
meat & rain dodging each other.

3 I love "laid-back." That burgundy
curtain is really laid-back. She
was in my arms on the scatological
sofa, & the music was, you know, laid-back.

4 You pull the ants from the somber
dominoes, & rattle off a history of
headstones, hitherto unknown to this
vexing section of the map.

5 We are washing out our best underwear
for the funeral.

THE LAST TIME I SAW PARIS

1 The bullfrogs had landed safely.
They were carefully gnawing their
way up some one-way streets. They

had invested wisely in tunics. The
weather, & all the surroundings gave
an inkling of an inhabited country.

You boarded a train with a pass that
would last you as long as your heart
desired.

2 You had magnificent glands. They were
swollen, & hot. I furnished them with
cotton, I believe, is the way you say

it. You were not shortchanged, you
know. You made out quite well, after
all. Your eyes were quilted, & had

lost some of their recent brilliance.
You sat outside a stupid church in
a sweat shirt, reciting your travel plans.

3 You translated a long night song.
The birds continue to crackle in
the trees here, I may never come

again. We have all invested wisely
in tunics. A small red dog putters
into the sweat shirt, & creates a drama

of high proportions. Do not frame
your mind with loose stools; do not
figure you have anything coming.

THE ANIMALS OF THE NIGHT

Ate the ruined wheat. It was excess,
it was what we had.
                                        They lay down
near the fire, nodding nodding
to whatever was brought up.
                                                    They thought
the water was horse piss, that
bedding must be a quiet scream.
                                                         We
could not feel them out, we could not
sit next to them long.

ON BEING LOVESICK

1 I hike up my pants &
head for Trenton. As I pass
the salt flats, the sky boils
with your eyes. & the red splats
near my feet, & the white coils
in the corner of my dull hand.

2 I have cut out sections,
counties in the ceiling; they
bulge with your fingers. Some
evenings, I pop open a beer, &
eat my way to a constellation,
a rough foot.

3 I cover the cold dog, & every
night he passes out.

THE WEEK OF THE HAYWIRE RAZOR

FOR N. N.

I am speechless. I have cut into
the Adam's apple, & I try to face
the sloppy words which hiss out of
that slit. "Hold it." & I do,
& a sonnet drips into my hand like
a tired Band-Aid. I think of redoing
my entire body of work. I think of
the new shape my voice will take.
I think you could bleed to death
slicing the apples, preparing the seeds.
I think of the styptic pencil large
enough to close the wound of a useless rib.

DIARY OF THE SUNSHINE KID

FOR GARY GILDNER

March 15, 1978
Today is the first day of the rest of your life.
This is the piece of ad copy I turned in today.
The Atomic Energy Commission did not find this
funny. They don't want me around there much
anymore.

March 16, 1978
Last night I dreamed I was a potato in the potato
famine. My eyes were not even formed, & I died.
Some scruffy people, probably my grandparents, dug
me up, looked me over, & said, "Not enough
there for a decent French fry." I was pleased.
I woke & knew that I had resolved my dilemma about
being consumed by people. I also concluded that
a potato is either the root of all evil, or the
center of the universe.

March 17, 1978
I listened to the rock 'n roll radio all day, &
lost a tooth in a tuna fish sandwich. It was
good. I went with the flow, & can still
hear Tommy James & the Shondels echoing
in my mouth. I put the tooth under my pillow.

March 18, 1978
This morning, an ear infection. & I don't think
it's funny. Job interviewers do not respect
people with ear infections. Your penis can fall
off, & no one gets too hot about that, but an
ear infection is a true degeneracy. I went to
the fish doctor for some oatmeal & cookies.
He gave me a hard shot in the ear, & one in the
mouth. I'm boiling, burning up.

KREPLAP SHOPS

Kreplap shops for himself
on basketball courts, in a
basket of discontinued wines, he
shops in the windows, he shops.

"If I have a nickel & I give it
to that good friend, the one
with Styrofoam eyes, & soybean
nose, & everything works out
in the end, I'll fly off

the handle, lose myself in the
geography of Sweden, & eventually
wind up without my white legs. It
isn't necessary to agree with

tentacles of bones, or vascular contractions,
but clumsy song
inside my throat, I want to give
it back, cut it out,

& work my way across the water."

KREPLAP, TO THE CLEANERS

Kreplap hauls his pants
to the cleaners. A pair
of strawberry cones, twelve
hundred cherries on toothpicks. "Kick
city, & the llamas of the night." There
is a pause, he is crossing a street
with great difficulty. The legs of
the pants are atom smashers, & it is
nearly noon. "I
like the fit, & I like the nap;
the color is another bruise below
the kneecap. Suppose your real
good friend came up from behind you,
& with his karate hand caught you
in the ligaments, the tendons, you
fold up, you hit your knee
on the sidewalk." He has made
it.

KREPLAP PRIES OPEN THE BOX

He comes back, a broken room, &
call it home. For the moment,

he is brushing his teeth, playing
in the deodorant. I want to pass

him up. Brush the dusk from my
desk. Open up a wine factory

in his heart. He breathes like a mother
in a dark & serious home. I spot him

ten balls; we go on. Praise each other
for our tools, our gifts. He tells me

the old one, how you must feel
the kinks, the spine, the boxcars, the

freezers on their way north. Oh wealth,
bone dust swelling in our heels.

KREPLAP BOILS OVER IN THE MOVIES

Someone is sitting in his seat.
Someone holding a box of popcorn

in his crotch. He sits behind his
seat. He takes off his white
trench coat, slips it over the body

sitting in his seat. He hears, breath,
bones whining, sighing. "It was about
some people who find a landing barge

in New Mexico. They didn't know
how to fix it. So they just left
it alone, & thought about it, & the

heat kept them going. It was about
silence, & dentistry. Someone needed
that tooth pulled, & no one could

do that without screams. It was a
fire in the projection room, & the
new junior high school was in there with

the man in the T-shirt. They were playing
with matches. Their fingers burped. I
felt like a spy. I drank vodka, & kept

my mouth shut. It was the smart thing
I was going to do. I put my file away,
& do not think I got out unharmed. The

curtain & my coat are in bad shape. I
cannot hope for spot remover or the
end of pictures like this. If someone

could keep me company, my elbows would relax.
I could be a pack of cigarettes, I could be
someone's steady friend."

KREPLAP STEPS OUT

It was not the drinking yourself
blind, or the trial-boss clothing.

Or the marzipan. The windows were
closed, & it was getting hot enough,

I think, to tell the time. Burning
your brains out with friends

in a place like the Rainbow Grill.
Someone noticed something & said

something else. The words were
hip huggers. & I don't remember

anything to eat. Small families
with nothing on the table to share.

I remember trying to care
a great deal, & not wanting you

to improvise late at night after
everything else was closed. You did not

hear me say as I did, "This is the
last cruel life I will live."

Selections From *The Reader's Digest* Series

THE MYTH OF THE VANISHING FAMILY

The family is sitting in the living room.
They look pretty bored. With father
leading the way, they climb into the
television set, all nine children, mother.
They look out at us, & smile for about
ten years.

WHY WORKING AT SEX DOESN'T WORK

I've been collecting unemployment
for the last couple of years, & I
rather enjoy it.

CRISIS IN MIDDLE EAST OIL

A can of heavy-duty oil was sitting in
the Middle East, getting a suntan, & eating
some grape leaves. He wasn't thinking about
being in a foreign country, since there is
no foreign country for a can of oil. He
was reading a sloppy book about inflation,
& the end of the world's natural resources.
Well, that's the way he got his rocks off,
& everything's o.k., as long as you don't
push it too far. The grape leaves made him
fart, but he figured that's o.k., everything
farts once in a while. Of course, oil cans
shouldn't fart. They leave the air a little
like Gary, Indiana. & the paint peels off
the cars in two, maybe, three hours, so that
people in places like that do nothing but
paint cars all the time. Heavy Duty, also,
had a weak bladder, an inherited trait, which
went over like a dirty joke with the town
counsel of this particular piece of sand.
Without getting too far afield, they pushed
a church key into his head, & broke his
sunglasses. His allegiances were divided.
He liked the sun, but he didn't like getting
burned or opened up to the point where you're
vulnerable to anything including air, hash,
water, or broken valves. It was a short
trial: "Are you now, or have you ever been,
a crisis?" "*Nolo contendere.*"
It didn't take them long to send him away
for life.

MIRACLE OF THE FLOWER BOXES

You were growing toward the sun, some-
body told you that was the thing to do,
so, that's where you headed. Each morning
you had that one thing in mind, & it
looked like it was brought up well. No
starving in weak soil; no waiting for
the water. One of my favorite jokes:
An angel & a friend of hers climb this
tree with this anchor, & what they do with
this anchor, they bake it in thirteen
languages, & they ask the anchor about
its heritage. & the anchor says, "I
was born where they rust hearts, &
your eyes bulge with insincerity. I
was born where they think of you as
a little willow, or a seedling. I was
born where noodle pudding was supposed
to solve everything, & it nearly did."
& then, the tree said, "What the hell's
a flower box, what the hell's an angel,
& is a miracle like a boned fish?"

I AM JANE'S OVARY

"She went over Sally's, & won't be
back for a while. But sit down, put
your feet up, you dirty fruitcake, you
wizard of plastic lawns. One day, Jane
says, 'What you want to be when you grow
up?' & I says, 'Why, a carhop, a brain wave,
a lean-to, or maybe, just an ovary.' But
see, Sally's the other one, & Jane spends
more time over there. & she leaves me
with all the rotten records, *Slaughter
On Tenth Avenue, The Stroll, The Hand Jive,*
& icky stuff like that. But I have ways
of getting back, you know what I mean?
Sometimes I take a little snooze for two
or three months at a stretch."

WHY SOME WOMEN RESPOND SEXUALLY & OTHERS DON'T

She wears good clothes. Her best. She
has driven herself crazy, driving the
Imperial to town. She's squeezing the
Charmin, & now she's squeezing the
melons. Nothing's ripe. You can
see this in her eyes. She gives the
quotes from today's American Stock Exchange.
She buys a kayak, floats down the Housatonic
River, & throws Charmin rolls, & melons
at the people who have gathered for
the fireworks.

POEMS FOR OTHERS

They are no more difficult
than lying to your mother.

Passing a brain cell on to a
captured duck. Look, his feathers

are matted. He has only one eye.
He doesn't enjoy his feet. He shits

in the street. I will dine out tonight,
a ripple in a shallow trout stream.

All my friends glazed, dead, or
limping to a silent table.

THE PROCESS

"The man without teeth should talk
about corn cobs, & things of that nature."
—Lum Kertile, *Lumping It All*

Last Saturday night, I heaved
up a part of my life I rarely
get to see. It was yellow, a
reminder of the suicidal crayfish,
contaminants, braces, & moving
scissors in my stomach.
"You little
prick, you're a coward, & you'll move
out." Or else.

That night I wanted to sleep upstairs,
& wake early, & get going on a poem.
A comedian kept me awake with a joke
about an anchor, an anchor, an anchor.

"This is the last time you'll make
this nose bleed." I have no excuses
my hands were taught early, & at home.
Keep them moving & no one will ever
touch you.
"Kill yourself," she
said. The knives of sun
drop down, drop down. I will
be there when they do. A dirty
yellow sheet, a crumpled note
stuck in my stomach.

BURNING THE BUSH

FOR MY BROTHER

The moon was not as talented as we thought
driving thru the Sinai like wax merchants.

You only need books when the voice is gathered
in a bad stitch.

This stretch of land is covered with the blossoms
of cucumbers. The vines tangle with the residue
of light.

I poke thru the ashes of the sun. I recall
the dirty snakes in the forest humming my name.

ODE TO MY TONSILS

I hear boils stretched out
in the snow. There was nothing
the roots slowed up, collapsed,

whiskers in the speech, the sun
that goes down. We have been
tampering, training, & my daughters

egg me on, they want naming, nodding,
a line of fences in the sunset, what
names, who has a name like that? The

tonsils are not pleasing women, when they speak
the Spanish, & their skins brood, I
would put all my hands into their hearts.

The things slip out of hand, the broken
windows of tonsils croon on, which
piece of dirt breeds infection, what

light is shed on the coiling fingers?
Pain was a hair or two out of place.
Pain was a mother with two teeth missing.
Pain was the open mouth of fire.

A FOLK SONG

FOR LINDA

My woman & her wishbone, I repeat,
my woman & her wishbone, dry
their hair in the gnarling sun.

It was not salad in the eyes of
the world. They took the land like
mongrels with signs that said, "Over

the river, & thru the woods to Grandmother's
house, we go." I'm not going there
& we slobber on the shallow road, seeing

who can spit, who can fabricate a stream
with their own blood. I was dreaming
again last night, oh honey, the building

with blue spires was sold for seventy-five
fish, count them, seventy-five. Each time
I reached into my pocket to count out the

bills, lambs, lambs are not smackers, &
where could I go from there. I hold my
famous poleax, it belongs to an ex-

student who wanted me to see the weapons
shining in his room. I took this pole-
ax, & did some damage to his collection.

A valuable lesson can be learned, even tho
we eat the spring chicken as tho he were a
diced rat, we can look at the book of

strange fucks with an open eye, almost
as if we were there when it all took
place. I give nothing up, I crouch down

in my chair & pass out the pencils, "Write
your name at the top, & if you have to piss,
hold it." Yesterday, quite seriously, a

tired wasp landed on my arm, a pea, a small
one, in his mouth. It was a choice, take the
pea back to the hungry kids or suck a little

weak blood from my arm. Oh I knew
the wasp's answer, tho I didn't know
what I would have done. Random sampling

would get us somewhere if we had any
needs. But there you are, no one to
hold you but yourself, & you do that,

after you go for the mail, & several
gallons of gas, & a couple of next
week's lottery tickets, apple juice,

& the local newspaper. As that American
poultry critic once said, "This guy
writes what's at the front of his head."

He was not kidding. So you slide off
into a haze of Milk Duds, & you buy back
last year's tools. You speak in the voice

of the late candidate, "I been to the doctor,
I know what it is, a dwarf swimming the
Atlantic, from North to South. It is no

secret what God can do. What he's done
for me, he can do for you." The willow
rides out the storm in the arms of its

mother. The blue ant slithers across
the carpet; its head tucked close to
its apparent body. Give it a whirl,

it's no fun there in the belly of the
copperhead, tho the weather is good, clear,
never a cloudy day in this part of the

country. Dressing up to go downtown, rustle
up a quick bologna sandwich, & a double-
shot of Wild Turkey, no water. A slim

woman carries her body before your chuckling
eyes, you have nothing to say, except, "Please
shut off the jukebox." Her bodyshirt, you

did not know it was a bodyshirt tucked
in, you thought it was an orange blouse
which clung like hunger in a bad movie, now,

you clutch, you clutch her arm, "You look
like my sister; she's a nurse." You take
out your bongos, bang out a tune of rough

passion, she responds, like a two-tone
Ford, kicking you in the balls, upsetting
everything. You deserved it, you were

tapping out some wild things with your
fingers, & you know where that gets
you. Someplace near the end of the evening

you hold a No Parking sign in your arms,
not only do you cling to it, you set up
a stand, "Come on in, & see the Great

Fucks, & the Bad Scars, Scares that'll
chase your blues away." You come upon
your own lost country, my woman & her

wishbone we climb the best tree
in this country of crags. Oh where
have we been in the long time before?

THE BANISTER

What was it, made
us, in those newels,
those choice wooden
spider snarls, prowl
the stairs. They are

shaking themselves, each
other as they face up
to the hardwood. I can
hear them, lately,

in the skylights. The
night does not bother them.
They twist out of their
nests; come to rest

in my dirty hair. I am
leading you toward the torn
bedclothes. I am watching
you pause, smartly, at
each dark step.

SYMMETRY

The stickpin in the gold cushion
creeps up on you. Every night you

walk thru the veins in the wall.
Every night the wall staggers having come

in contact with you, sweetheart.

THE HANGNAIL

FOR CHARLES SIMIC

Some morning we will reach
with fingers
for our lovers, & there they

will be. Everything becomes
them. The time clocks, torches
of lambskin, we welcome back the sun.

I'm happy to say, I will never have
to wake again. This sawing dream,
clear cut,

a hangnail. It is too late to speak
English. It is too late to return
collect calls. I want to die

stroking fire.

THE SCENARIO

FOR DAVE KELLY

Should we ever clean up the despair,
the darkness in that room,
some bastard would fly from our bodies,

& scream a thousand savage dreams:
I am praying for dimes in the gutter.
A cow steps on my head. I sing now
for nickels, or for anyone with ears.

No one was bitter there. They all tasted
like wheat. A resurrection of guilt.
I lose a piece of thumb trying
to throw aside the broken Coke bottles.

My ex-wife drills a hole thru the wall
with her finger. She throws a *moue*, &
expects undivided attention. I Spackle
that hole; pass two red cards to the left,
one to the right. Anaconda.

For three full days, they renovate the brownstone
next door. No one sees any reason to it.
A man in glad rags, a silver-haired devil,
steps out of the Imperial into the sun,
pointing like a dark field dog. "How are
things going, boys?" He is the father
of this impending doll house.

These *no ones* return as if they were starlings.
A momentary birth of one cell. I hang on
with this rough chest, & let the rest probe
with kits they have concocted for their kids.
Their one-winged birds flap in the cool sand, cooing.

This is not *cinéma vérité*, or a winch in the spine.
This is a note to a long-lost friend, tearing
hair out, pretending there is a world that can
be easily removed.

FURTHER EDUCATION

Compound sentences run on
thru the nursery—they pump
feathers at the catalpa trees
plastered to the calm walls.

A French verb murmurs in the hall.
I feel as if I am in the vagina of
this special French verb, & she
understands Magic Fingers, & a morning
restaurant where people you know
show up, & call you by name.
You may now order breakfast.

Most pieces of language, helpless
loons in a tree house, no one to
feed them, to introduce them to
distant relatives, who might in turn,
if they were getting along with that
side of the family, introduce them
to other foreign relatives. We would
beat the incest, or the blood
would grow so thin we'd be pumping gas
for lifetimes.

I kiss the frail stomach of this verb
good night. I will take in her tongue
next week, & she will learn the true
life adventures of waterfalls, acorn
squash, broken espresso machines,
& the tooth that would wear any
of this foolish clothing.

"I was there for six years." But she
would not talk about her imprisonment
& cried mentioning it.

FOUR LIVES

I did not eat my cereal, or my toast
with the poached egg. I ate, instead,
the oil of sardines, & I did, indeed,

like all of them I encountered. I
walked into the stomach you seem to
hold so dear. What a strange way

to bring up the children. The things
in my mouth hurt more than the things
they took out. I could have been

lonely in an elephant's heart. I sought
favors from funny books. I lick, & a
strong man prints himself on my tongue.

A Candy-gram, hot-wired, practices
a couple of new chords, slightly below
my thigh. I am not used to this,

I am sure, you will understand, if I
cannot reply like the mezzo-soprano
warming up in the back room of this

diner.

CRAWLING OUT YOUR MOUTH

I am not a tear in the heart of the newspaper.
I am not a figment of the loony midget's voice.

I am not a carol in the middle of a national holiday,
or the borscht on the country table. I am not

the canyon, the random dampness in the cellar.
I am close to everyone with ears. I am your

regular stalled car.

THE DEAD

I used my poems to read you off
to sleep. You went sliding thru
one of *The Lady Poems*. No one
moaned, or took them too seriously,
until our friends prowled, & found
the dead women, crowded together,
reunited on an old tuna ketch in
the North Atlantic.

KAPOK

I am dreaming the rubble
of my cock, & the cities.
Buying new land in the morning.

I look to Shelley at my age, &
he was relaxing in some knuckle
country. Lucifer unlocking his

whipcord trousers, grinding out our
last cigarette of the evening.

MAKING THE POEM

& now I am so crazy I cannot
write a line without worrying,
am I fucking it up already?

& this is only the first line,
& I have watched every probing
doctor story on T.V., & I'm right

back where I began, my mother's tomb,
thumping, weeping, wiggling the little
toes of my words.

THE SLICK PAGE

1 There are years you sit down.
Whatever falls from the clouds, passes

through you, onto a slick page. It seems
that simple, sometimes. Then,

the potted plant starts its dying, roots
soaked, nothing props you up.

You sleep to keep from smoking. You
smoke to bind yourself to the dark

ashtray. Your fingers get spooked,
the coy twists of light in letters.

How to continue without wicker,
without self-starting keys, or

warm water? How seriously do you
take yourself? & where?

2 This page slips out of the machine,
wanders around in the clucking

street. Breaks into a gas station,
breaks into a candy machine, & leans

on a fat clean car. I cannot speak
to this language, I cannot get

involved. Is this obvious? Is
that the way it goes? When I signed

up for this fun-filled vacation, I was
guaranteed desire, hot knees, & slow

aches in groin. This slip
of paper rolls around, around

like a cluttered machine with a cranky
large intestine.

LAMENTS WITH THE BLACK DOG IN THE ROOM, SCRATCHING

FOR DAVID IGNATOW

And this is the library where I trim my cigar,
& hot-wire my life. They are perfect as I
stroke them with the red pulp of my tongue.
I certainly hope we cement our relationship
with Cuba, shortly. I have lost my touch, I have
lost my taste.

*   *   *

Having found cruelty, the closest I will ever
come to the evangelist, I slap the Bordeaux
glass on the table. Days later, the white walls
leak as if a swimmer were on the other side
scraping his foot on a piece of exquisite coral,
the deep blue eyes of the evangelist croon.

*   *   *

Sleep robs you of your toes. There are diners
in the wings.

*   *   *

Out in the streets, they are "motherfucking" this
or that. It does no good. It is too late.

*   *   *

I will sleep thruout the morning, drawing
in the dreams of the black dog, locked
on the couch.

*   *   *

I can hear my nails multiply. Tear open
the material world. I reconstruct coal
bins in my quiet heart.

THE DISHES

FOR GEORGE CHAMBERS

I remember doing them, or writing
about them. Doing them, perhaps
I was watching a soap commercial,
& I have done nothing at all. The
plants died one Thursday. Oh, I know
that. Worms or the dog. It was the peat
packed around the begonias. I liked most
of what I saw except the broken stems. &
none of this gets close to the fingernails,
chewed like the cusp of someone's horoscope.
I am pawing through dead men's mail. Pawing
& scratching, & I'm going to take this beer
to bed, & this pen, & some cigarettes, a couple
of catalogues, & most of the defenseless
people of the world. Tomorrow, I'll take to
heart the dishes, as dirty as they may be
by then.

NOODLE PUDDING

The chicken is bloody, & I won't
touch it. I will bleed, but I
will not eat the chicken

crying at the bone. However, I
will eat the red chicken before
I will have a spoonful of the

noodle pudding with its kind
stump stretching for a
subtle touch.

I WOULD COIL UP

& thank the coiling. The needle
pines settle. Dumb rocks cringe.
I have been happier in decent water.

The water of sober crime. Is it the
end? The mutant hospital? When you
reach into the fish pond, always,

returning home, what do you bring?
Call ahead? Or leave well enough
alone. The good friend huddles

in the corner, you think, the good
friend, & you are wrong. You wouldn't
know a song if it fell right out

of your wicked face.

THE FONDUE WEDDING RITUAL

FOR RUSSELL EDSON

We were given small brass pots, I thought,
perhaps to piss in. Then, with some verve
they passed out the lean, two-pronged fork
of love. Then the questions: Where's the
fire? Do you have any eye shadow? Is this
the only kettle of fish?

There is not even a word for what they
expected from us next. "Fondue, my wife,
Fondue, will take the bear trap from her
vagina, if you have any balls, or wish to
have any left, hold it, kiss it, & pass it on,
as we snap these candid shots of our first &
last wedding."

HAD WE BUT BALLS ENOUGH, & LIMES

Granting you several apples, the
woman then proceeds to
eat them like limes. It is
nothing new. It is
nothing, you didn't already
envision. She has come
lugging the broken people like
slugs for the phone with the bleeding mouthpiece.
Overtly, you pine for her as she
nods at your slim ankles.

CLEANING THE LEAVES

Vivaldi's splashing out of the small radio.
It is raining. It is summer. The season
of brine, & flatulence.

I am herding cattle toward Chicago.
I am draining the trees of their spikes.
I am hogging the whole trail.
I whimper in your old ear.

Last night the veal was tender.
You made a wonderful sauce. The
president quit. He left hoof prints
all over the bathroom.

I curl up near the refrigerator.
I finish the thousand-year-old roach.

THE DAY THE REFRIGERATOR FROZE OVER

I was humming along like a dangling modifier.
I hadn't yet discerned my needs. I knew
I had had too much gin, & country music.

I knew something powerful was fretting thru
the extra rooms. I knew I needed something
like a toothpick, or a carrier pigeon.

I braced myself against the bookshelf
for the intrusion. I do this quite often;
I wedge myself between *The Flowers of Evil,*

& some plastic hydrangeas. I knew I was
finally discovering a new language, words
a codfish in a freezer knew at birth.

FISH PAPER

1 Today, I papered the walls. Re-
papered the walls. Today, with
fish. Small fish from the supermarket.
Dead ones. Carpet tacks. Behind their
eyes. It is as if a pond had been turned
on its side. & I can see them swim in
slow motion. I have never had anything
like this before. I am quite happy. All
of their mouths are open. When they get
hungry I will feed them. Some I will use
as flower holders, their smiling mouths,
their mouths that speak with flowers. For
the ones who cannot speak, pencils, & pens.
I will fill them with pens.

2 They sag a little, their bellies, their
eyes, their gullets. It is as if they
did not live good, bloated with carbo-
hydrates. I do not know if the carpet
tacks will hold them. Their scales scream
when I pound large nails thru them, scream
& shatter. It gives me a headache in
my bones. They have eyes in their stomachs
where the big nails rest.

3 Today, in lust & hunger, I baked
one wall of wallpaper. A few cloves,
a few cloves of garlic, two slices of
orange. Paprika for color. Similar
to fish in newspaper. The erasers
melted. I like to think of the X-rays,
I will appear to have a chest full
of Atlantis. It is a dream world
I will fill up with glowing temples.
I have given myself some bread &
wine, I am swelling, & have very little
room left.

THE WRISTWATCH

1 My woman gave me a watch that has
a piece of blood floating around
the dial, counting a pulse, a second.

2 I grew up in the country. When
the sun moved, you noticed it.
When the sun moved, you moved, or
died, like gums succumbing to trench mouth.
Getting wasted is an early country tradition.

3 His heart is a glass harmonica.
He sees Ben Franklin introducing it
to Mozart. Ben says, "It's like the
bifocals; it takes a little while
to get used to." Wolfgang, an inkling
he has only a few months to wind up
the trembles of this earth, "Time
is not a thing you fuck around with;
I want to turn every second into a year
of resonances. Every second is a brain cell
screaming at its father. Think of
The Original Amateur Hour."

4 I have never been a tyrant of sound or vision.
Crumbling, a bridge might thunder into
the Mad River. I would never say
that was the end of the world, or the bookie
who ran the Cigar Store, & drove his
fragile car into the center of the flood,
"I'll get thru; the phones start jangling
at 7:50, & that's just the Big A."

5 Blood spot on the blue yolk, slip
your friends a tired hand. Blood spot
on the moon, give your friends
a deep, sweet kiss good night.

A NOTE ABOUT THE AUTHOR

Terry Stokes was born in 1943 in Flushing, New York, and grew up in a small town in the northwestern corner of Connecticut. He is a graduate of the University of Hartford and has an M.F.A. degree in Creative Writing from the University of Iowa. From 1971 through 1975 he was Poet-in-Residence at the University of Hartford, and in 1974 he received a grant from the Creative Artists Public Service Program. *Boning the Dreamer* is Mr. Stokes's third collection of poetry; *Natural Disasters* appeared in 1971 and *Crimes of Passion* in 1973. His poems have also been published in *Esquire, The New Yorker, American Poetry Review,* a number of small press collections, and as broadsides and postcards. He is now living in New York City and teaching in the City's Poets-in-the-Schools Program.

A NOTE ON THE TYPE

The text of this book was set in ELECTRA, a Linotype face designed by W. A. Dwiggins (1880–1956), who was responsible for so much that is good in contemporary book design. Although much of his early work was in advertising and he was the author of the standard volume *Layout in Advertising*, Mr. Dwiggins later devoted his prolific talents to book typography and type design and worked with great distinction in both fields. In addition to his designs for Electra, he created the Metro, Caledonia, and Eldorado series of type faces, as well as a number of experimental cuttings that have never been issued commercially.

Electra cannot be classified as either modern or old-style. It is not based on any historical model, nor does it echo a particular period or style. It avoids the extreme contrast between thick and thin elements that marks most modern faces, and attempts to give a feeling of fluidity, power, and speed.

This book was composed, printed and bound by American Book–Stratford Press, Inc., Brattleboro, Vermont. The typography and binding design are by Gwen Townsend.

In this new collection Terry Stokes extends the range of both his poetic material and his poetic manner. His last book, *Crimes of Passion*, presented a poetry of strange combinations: violence and amused detachment, a skittery kind of panic mixed with an even, assured playfulness. *The New York Times* called it "brash and busy as city streets," and spoke of the poet himself as "half altar boy, half sophisticate, a plebeian wary of literary culture [with] a genial, funky sensibility." The poems in *Boning the Dreamer* are marked by a more complex vision and a more finely tempered artistry while moving with the same brilliant bold ease.

The voice is coolly modulated, subtly varied. At times it is fast, snappy—the talk of an impatient friend: "I was humming along like a dangling modifier. / I hadn't yet discerned my needs. I knew / I had had too much gin, & country music." At times it is close and mournful: "My family, when clearly mapped, / dangles like a ghost-flower on a cactus. / . . . stooped people picking / potatoes, first in Ireland, then, miraculously, / from the cool sand of Long Island." And it can be wistful, whimsical, hinting a tenderness inside the tough-guy stance: "I'm going to take this beer / to bed, & this pen, & some cigarettes, a couple / of catalogues, & most of the defenseless / people of the world."

The poems powerfully evoke fleeting or lingering states of mind—waiting for a twin sister to "come home from that long / sexy date, & hold me in your arms"; refusing a noodle pudding "with its kind / stump stretching for a / subtle touch"; seeing death approaching "like a second-story man": "First, he cases the joint, / then, as